The School Year 180 Days Self-Care Challenge

By Renita Perry M. Ed

ISBN-13: 978-1727142655
ISBN-10: 1727142659

Dedication

WP & MP my first teachers

KB keeps me on my toes

JH listens, advises, and saves me money

KC &CS my critical love team

Acknowledgements

Thank you to my Heavenly father for blessing me with gift of creativity and ordering my steps.

Thanks to my family for your love, encouragement, and support.

To my family and friends thank you for motivating me and reminding me only what you do for Christ will last. I am grateful, humbled, and thankful for all of you. In the words of Marvin Sapp "I Never Would Have Made It Without You!"

Smooches

The School Year 180 Days Self-Care Challenge

By Renita Perry M. Ed

Table of Contents

Introduction

Self-care for Educators was a hot topic in the year 2018. Now in 2022, it is a hot topic for all professions. Many educators are stressed out, leaving the profession and even going to counseling for job related stress. This is not what I or my colleagues signed up for when we choose to become people who help and guide the future.

The education professional has changed drastically over the last seven years with demands on accountability, increase work load with lack of resources, reduced funding, and high stakes testing. Not to mention children are coming to school with health concerns, exposure to traumatic experiences, and basic needs not being met.

The 2020 Pandemic caused a rise in job changes, loss of wages, food insecurity, working from home, using virtual platforms for meetings and teaching, plus worship services. Some people had to learn a new skill set in order to maintain their same job. Life changes and uncertainties were all around twenty-four seven.

Educators are also spending their own monies to ensure their students are having quality learning experiences, supplying gloves and hats, and sometimes gift cards when families have run out of food.

Educators have been defined as caring, helpful, loving, loyal, responsible, nurturing, and reliable to name a few.

Those are the traits that led educators and people in serving professions to taking care of everyone else but themselves. Therefore, self-care is at the end of the list.

Self-care is the one way to increase your joyful and abundance lifestyle.

Spouse, children, parents, siblings, cousins, in-laws, and students are placed at the top of the list. In my belief system, only God should be placed before you. Sadly, that is not the case. Educators have placed themselves under everybody else including the family pet.

We make sure the family dog, Snow Baby Bella goes to the veterinarian, gets to the groomer, and does not run out of dog treats. As educators we have taken care of everybody and everything but ourselves.

That is not healthy to the mind, body, or soul. Often, we wait to the beginning of a new year to start a new routine, create a vision board for the year, or a bucket list. That philosophy stops as soon as you read this sentence, if that is you.

The purpose of this book is to help educators, teachers, nurses, custodians, bus drivers, administrators, counselors, para professionals, volunteers, administrative assistants, and, coaches to start increasing their life span by indulging in regular on-going self-care.

On going regular self-care is a must for the doctor, nurse, politician, mortician, counselor, athlete, lawyer, truck driver, accountant, scientist, computer programmer, pastor, and even the retired employee.

We were created to live an abundance, joyful, peaceful, harmonious, and wonderful life. Self-care is the twenty-first century way to maintain balance, peace, fulfillment, joy, happiness, calmness, balance, and gratitude in your life.

Are you willing to take on the 180-day School Year Self-Care Challenge?

"Remember to take care of yourself. You can't pour from an empty cup."
Unknown

Why Self-Care?

When flying on an airplane the voice overheads states, "in case of emergency, place the oxygen mask on yourself first if you are flying with small children." The field of aviation, including pilots, flight attendants, mechanics, air traffic controllers and reservationists understood the assignment of self-care.

Self-care has been defined as anything intentional in action taken to meet an individual's needs-mental, physical, emotional, and spiritual.

Translation, little things people do to take care of themselves to avoid breakdowns and meltdowns. Self-care can also be defined as activities and practices to reduce stress and take care of ourselves.

The definition of self-care is any action that you use to improve your health and well-being.

The National Institute of Mental Illness states there are six elements of self-care.

- Physical
- Emotional
- Psychological
- Professional
- Spiritual
- Social

Ideally a healthy self-care strategy should include an activity or activities that addresses all six elements every day.

In 2016, I began to experience numerous lives altering situations that I had no control over or could control. My job was eliminate causing me to experience sleepless night, headaches, and unhealthy eating habits. Not to mention I had begun daily job searching. Plus, I was being harassed in the work place. Then to add to the list a friend was relying on me for prayer for their family in the loss of their matriarch along with major damage from a tornado.

Later in the year my only living parent experienced a medical emergency that required hospitalization. Six weeks later, the family was informed by the doctor that my mother would not be able to live in her home independently and would need supervised around the clock care. I began searching for an assistant living apartment and cleaning out a home in preparation for a house sale.

To top off my stress, I was placed in a new assignment only five minutes from my home. However, in the words of TD Jakes it was a toxic work environment, which caused more stressed.

The medical profession commonly refers to them as major life stressors. I use to voice daily to my support group "I am one situation away from losing my mind." They replied pray about it, take a mental health day, go to the doctor and get some medicine, quit your job, etc. They gave good advice but it was not enough.

I was extremely busy and now responsible for taking care of everybody else's health, finances, schedules, problems, events, relationships, and wardrobe concerns. I forgot to encourage myself and participate in self-care for me.

 Mind you I was still taking care of my own finances, health, schedules, working full time plus coming home to my personal responsibilities along with running one small business and a contractor for another small business. I forgot to take care of my main priority self. Out of those experiences I started to realize taking care of myself is not selfish its selfless.

Fast forward it's now 2020. On March 18th, I began teaching 21 energetic elementary students from my home classroom virtually. A two week change in location status turned into12 weeks of teaching at home. August 2020, to March 2021, I taught a new group of students in a newly created classroom space in my basement. Virtual Teaching on Zoom for the first time ever

New experiences caused anxiety and uncertainty. Challenging year but it was in that season I realized I must do something for myself to stay calm and relaxed during the Pandemic.

To top things off my mother contracted COVID-19 in April 2020, and was admitted to the hospital on a Friday afternoon. Five days later she succumbed to COVID-19 and went to her eternal rest. Now I'm little orphan Renita, with more major life changes going on. By January of 2021, I lost numerous family members to COVID-19 and was still suffering from complications from a 2018 car accident.

I was on the verge of losing my mind and sought out professional help. The take away from all the major life changes was I needed to put myself first and practice self-care on a regular ongoing schedule to remain mentally, physically, emotionally, and spiritually healthy.

A wise person said that job you are working extra hard for will replace you before your burial, if you die. That job will replace you in a hot second.

However, to your family and friends you are irreplaceable. If you do not take care of yourself and love on yourself, why should anyone else? Everyone not only deserves self-care but needs it to thrive.

We know that self-care is an important element of wellness. What most of us struggle with is finding the time for self-care. Making time for self-care can be difficult when you've got work, school, side hustles, family, and somehow adding in a social life.

The problem with not making time for self-care is that, at some point, it's going to affect all of those other areas in your life. Sooner or later, you are going to be burnt out if you don't start prioritizing taking care of yourself first.

The good news is that self-care doesn't have to be a huge time commitment. Although, I do suggest doing activities like a nap, bubble bath, or even a massage from time to time. The truth is that self-care can be simple acts that let us allow us to prioritize ourselves.

"Self-care is how you take your power back."
Lalah Delia

Benefits of Self Care

Lack of self-care can lead to people being in a rut, wearing clothing that is too tight or too big, or eating on the go resulting in bad eating habits.

Those bad habits can lead to depression, low self-confidence, avoiding friends and family, meltdowns, emotional roller coasters of feelings, and on edge.

Self-care is a great way to reduce feelings of depression and disconnection with others to begin feeling better physical, mentally, emotionally, socially, and spiritually.

Improving self-care has benefits such as:

Your health and sleep improve
Stress level decreases
Possible weight lost
Your blood pressure might decrease
Energy level increases to enjoy things you like
You will feel better about yourself
Increase sex drive and time for love ones
Work performance increases
Sustained concentration and improves focus
Increases productivity
Creates motivation and work life balance
Manages anxiety
Increases self-awareness

Educating Today

As educators we teach children from diverse backgrounds and situations. Like children we have diverse backgrounds and experiences unique to each educator. However, sometimes we forget if the children we serve have experienced a traumatic situation and we are aware of it, witnessed it, read about it on social media, or visited the family for support we take on their trauma too.

Educators are underpaid and over worked. We are the only profession that has to purchase needed supplies to get the job done. We spend thousands of dollars to decorate and set up buildings supported by tax dollars. On an average day some educator is at home grading assignments, creating lesson plans, shopping for incentives, contacting parents, reading manuals to teach the next day's lesson, attending professional training all while their own family time is being shorten and their health status is declining.

Precious hours of sleep are shorter, meals are quick and fast, exercise is sometime non-existence due to being mentally and physically exhausted. Therefore, educators stress level can sometime be on overload.

Many educators express there is no teacher tired like end of the year tired or first week back to school tired. The point is teaching children in the 21st century is stressful and hazardous to your mental, physical, and emotional heath.

Selfcare is much needed in the education arena to prevent burnout, illness, and vacating the profession. As I was struggling with this issue I realized I was not alone in putting myself first and taking care of self.

"Take time to do what makes your soul happy." Unknown

Selfcare for Educators

I decided to compile a list of ways to indulge in self-care. Just recently Time magazine featured teachers on the front cover and how underpaid they are. I decided to include self-care ideas on a zero-dollar budget to an unlimited dollar budget.

I asked this question, what do you do for selfcare, in several social media groups of educators and non-educators in 2018. I asked the same question again in 2022. Two years after the Pandemic started and four years after 2018. Remember self-care is the best way to take care of yourself. A healthy selfish person can then help others and themselves.

The activities and practices in this text work for all people. Whether you are on a beer budget or champagne budget, there is something in this book that you can do for self-care. This guide was written with the educator in mind but we are all educators, for we have all taught someone something.

The purpose of me writing this book is to help guide and support my beloved educators and all working people who have jobs or careers to take better care of yourself. I want educators, to take time out and indulge in self-care throughout the school year not just Winter Break, Spring Break, or Summer Break. I want laborers and workers to take time and indulge in self care not just during vacation time.

Leave that teacher bag at school and start enjoying your time away from work with yourself, friends, and family.

These activities will help one take better care of themselves and live a healthy, well balanced, abundant selfish life.

Are you ready to start the 180 days Self- Care Challenge?

"The only person who can pull me down is myself, and I'm not going to let myself pull me down anymore."   C. JoyBell C.

Self- Care Ideas and Practices

Just for Educators

Check work email during working hours
Attend an Eddie B Comedy Show
Attend a Gerry Brooks Comedy Show
Leave on time everyday
Stay late one day a week for paperwork
Come early one day a week for paperwork
Leave that teacher bag at home
Plan time is for working not socializing
Schedule a regular restroom break
Drink water throughout the day
Listen to music on break
Play calming music when teaching
Teach students to grade their work
Utilize technology to reduce paper task
Make anchor charts at school
Plan fun activities for the students
Take random days off
Set boundaries at work
Display quotes that you like in your space.
Place pictures and objects that make you
smile in your area
Keep school email off your personal device
Take your lunch break
Eat a planned meal during your lunch break

Reply to work email during contractual time.
Consider working a little longer each day to save the evenings and weekends for yourself and social events with family and friends.
Keep healthy snacks at work to munch on
Bring fruit and vegetables to snack on
Play your favorite music during plan time.
Go outside and enjoy the fresh air.
Stay away from the school on weekends.
Plan 10-15 minutes to decompress.
Take a break away from everyone but YOU.
Walk the perimeter of the playground for exercise during lunch time.
Walk the hall before leaving work to get your steps in and to clear your head.
Bring your water bottle to work to encourage drinking plenty of water.
Take district issued computer home daily in case of an emergency virtual learning day.
Create generic guest teacher plans to leave on your desk before you need them.
Set quiet hours for parents when you do not respond to communications

"Don't get so caught up in being accessible to the world that you become inaccessible to your family." Anonymous

Just for Laborers & Workers

Listen to music
Read a book
Take a nap after work
Go to a movie
Visit a cultural site outside your city
Journey on a day trip
Pamper yourself
Relax
Eat chocolate
Exercise
Walk
Mediate
Keep in a Journal
Give up your routine for one night
Be spontaneous with love ones
Attend a concert
Attend a comedy show
Attend a play
Attend a recital
Attend a dance
Attend a musical
Attend a sporting event
Take a relaxing soaking bath
Go out on a date with yourself
Go out on a date with a significant other

Indulge in your favorite meal
Indulge in your favorite beverage
Get adequate sleep
Indulge in your passions
Indulge in your hobbies
Learn something new
Spend time with love ones
Play a game
Take a break from technology
Go on a nature walk
Admire nature
Devotional time
Read the Bible
Hangout with uplifting people
Go golfing
Swim laps
Learn to say no
Attend free movie screenings
Attend movies on discounted days
Create a quiet meditation space
Use your quiet meditation space
Buy yourself some flowers
Attend a car show with a buddy
Take a candle lit bath
Go to the beach and wave watch
Go to the beach and put feet in water
Make sandcastles at the beach
Write your favorite quote in the sand

Read a bestseller on the beach
Read a low seller on the beach
Walk along the coast on the beach
Say self-affirmations
Take a nice long bubble bath
Find and install a meditation app
Start better eating habits
Visit a therapist if needed
Watch a meditation video on You Tube
Attend a self-development class
Visit the library
Keep work and family life separate
Use Eventbrite to find free events
Drink 100 ounces of water
Visit estate sales
Find fresh produce at Farmers Markets
Letting go of a bad friend
Forgive self
Understanding you are worth it
Understanding your value
Prayer
Read in natural light
Take a mental health day off work
Self-appreciation day with a $25 budget
Dancing
Go walking by water
Go walking on a trail
Visit the zoo
Visit a working farm
Hiding in the library for two hours to read

Do something for yourself daily
Do something for yourself weekly
Do something for yourself monthly
Soak your feet while listening music
Play a game on your device
Walks in the mountain
Play tennis
Whale watching
Go Camping
Cook your favorite meal
Attend a cooking class with a buddy
Set goals and check off when accomplished
Use Groupon for discounts
Painting
Drawing
Play the guitar
Take guitar lessons
Volunteer
Find things you like to do and schedule them
Travel the world
Create a bucket list and do it
Binge watch your favorite show on Netflix
Listen to music on Pandora
Learn something new by watching You-Tube
Go fishing
Go sailing
Visit a new city
Buy flowers for an elderly friend
Clean out your closet and donate items
Visit a Farmers Market in your city
Write a poem

Catch up on a blog
Star gaze
Read a magazine
Read an E-book for free on a Kindle app
Get a new hair style
Play catch with a buddy
Jump rope
Go canoeing
Drink a glass of wine
Ride a bike
Take a cruise
Visit a winery
Go to a wine tasting
Visit a hot spring
Sew
Quilt
Quit a bad habit
Start a new morning routine
Knit
Crochet
Rearrange furniture in your house
Watch your favorite classic movie
Visit a museum
Visit a comedy club
Visit a National Park
Visit the Grand Canyon and take a selfie
Limit alcohol
Keep a gratitude diary
Watch a professional sports team play live
Go to the local high school sporting event
Attend your alma mater homecoming game

Unfollow a toxic "friend" on social media
Read your favorite children's book
Buy an adult coloring book and color
Paint on canvas
Go on a scenic drive
Take a short car ride
Take a day trip
Ride public transportation
Visit the Grand Canyon
Go hear a local band play
Visit Whole Food Market for a meal
Ride a motorcycle
Roller skate
Read a biography of someone you admire
Watch a video of someone famous on
Biography.com
Ice skate
Golf
Swim
Play tennis
Float Trip
Couponing
Karaoke
Praise God
Compose music
Arrange music
Watch HGTV
Play Candy Crush
Laugh with friends
Walk during lunch break
Eat tons of sushi

Forgive yourself
Take yourself out on a date
Meal prep for the week
Spend time outdoors
Sunbathe
DIY project for the home
DIY project for fun
DIY project for the holiday
Host a game night
Install Word Connect App then play it
Play Words with Friends
Visit a waterfall
Play with grandkids
Go to Sam's Club for the free samples
Visit the Football Hall of Fame
Visit the Baseball Hall of Fame
Visit the Pony Express Museum
Create a vision board
Execute your plan on your vision board
Take a noneducational online class
Go sledding
Play in the rain
Build a snowman with someone or solo
Check into a local hotel for a staycation
Take a dinner boat cruise
Take a dinner train ride
Plant a flower garden
Go to a local fair
Visit Restaurant Week in your city
Schedule a couple massage
Create a playlist of your favorite song

Get a facial
Work in the garden if you have one
Update your wardrobe
Sleep in
Cook a nourishing meal for yourself
Visit a new country
Explore a cave
Take a relaxing bubble bath with candles
Go to the spa
Watch a sunset or sunrise
Keep a gratitude journal
Write something you are thankful daily
Spend time doing an old hobby
Visit Alaska on a trip
Create a Bucket List
Cook something new for a meal
Attend a Professional Sporting event
Have quiet time
Go get your hair, nails, and feet done at a
technical college, cheaper than a salon
Drink tea with pajamas on wrap in a blanket
Buy ice cream with the children in the family
Walk before leaving work to get steps in
Walk before leaving work to clear your head
Reach out to an old friend
Eliminate a sugary beverage for water
Soak your feet while watching your favorite
movie
Go to the library to read your favorite type of
book

Go to a therapist
Sleep in
Hang out with animals
Create a new playlist
Do Taiichi
Take an online class at Michaels
Take a cooking class with a buddy
Redesign your room
Play video games
Make a scrapbook
See a live show
Do a puzzle
Plant a garden
Pick apples at an orchard
Take a hayride in Fall
Play a board game
Go outside and watch the clouds
Visit a bookstore and browse
Eat your favorite dessert
Visit Hollywood Walk of Fame
Go up in the Gateway Arch in Missouri
Create a self-care emergency kit to bring to
work with items you enjoy so you can destress
when needed
Use self-care apps
    Stop Breathe & Think
    Drink Water Reminder
    Moodpath
    I am
    Gratitude
    Colorfy
    Calm
    White Noise Lite

Self-Care Ideas A to Z

- ✓ Arts & Crafts or Adult Coloring Book
- ✓ Binge watch a series on a Streaming App
- ✓ Couch and wine or Calming App
- ✓ Daily Devotion or Disconnect from social media
- ✓ Every weekend do something you love
- ✓ First hour of waking up pray, meditate, exercise
- ✓ Garage Sales or Game Time on your device
- ✓ Hike or Horseback Riding
- ✓ Ice Fishing
- ✓ Jewelry Making
- ✓ Kick boxing or Kite Flying
- ✓ Lift weights
- ✓ Massage or Meditation App
- ✓ It's ok to say NO
- ✓ Ocean visit
- ✓ Put yourself first,
- ✓ Quilling, or Quilting
- ✓ Relax, Read, or Rise early to see a sunrise
- ✓ Solo Trip, Spa, or Scuba Dive
- ✓ Travel to a place you always wanted to visit
- ✓ Unicycle Lessons
- ✓ Visit the doctor
- ✓ Window Shop
- ✓ eXpress gratitude daily
- ✓ Yoga
- ✓ Zumba

Quotes on Self-Care

"The most powerful relationship you will ever have been the relationship with yourself."
Steve Maraboli

"Self-compassion is simply giving the same kindness to ourselves that we would give to others."
Christopher Germer

"Lighten up on yourself. No one is perfect. Gently accept your humanness." Deborah Day

"You must love yourself before you love another. By accepting yourself and fully being what you are, your simple presence can make others happy."
Unknown

"You may encounter many defeats, but you must not be defeated. Please remember that your difficulties do not define you. They simply strengthen your ability to overcome." Maya Angelou

"If you don't love yourself, nobody will. Not only that, you won't be good at loving anyone else. Loving starts with the self."
Wayne Dyer

"Almost everything will work again if you unplug it for a few minutes, including you."
Anne Lamott

Self-Affirmations

Affirmations are short powerful statements used to challenge unhelpful thoughts. Build confidence and positive self-talk with affirmations. Speak affirmations aloud to yourself daily as part of your morning/evening routine. Write them on sticky notes and place around your space for a visual reminder

- ✓ My challenges help me grow
- ✓ I deserve peace and joy in my life
- ✓ Every day is a chance to start fresh
- ✓ Your opinion of me is not my reality
- ✓ Asking for help is a sign of strength
- ✓ I am more than enough
- ✓ I am not afraid to try new things
- ✓ I accept myself the way I am
- ✓ I am fearfully and wonderfully made
- ✓ I am loved, loving, and lovable.
- ✓ I am blessed
- ✓ I choose joy
- ✓ I take a few minutes to relax each day
- ✓ I do simple things to make me happy
- ✓ I choose to be happy
- ✓ I choose to be thankful
- ✓ I am thankful, grateful, and blessed
- ✓ I am capable
- ✓ I am strong
- ✓ I am resilient
- ✓ I value my worth

Endnotes

Research states it takes twenty-one to sixty-six days to develop a new habit and the old adage it takes twenty-one days to break a habit is a myth.

The idea behind this book is the reader will take better care of themselves by using some of the ideas presented in the book. My hope is after reading this book educators, laborers, and workers including myself will take the time to care for themselves daily with some sort of self-care activity or practice.

Remember selfcare is the best care. Taking care of self is not selfish its selfless! Put your oxygen mask on first. Self-care is necessary to maintain good mental health. Self-care can be a way to prevent or cure stress.

In true teacher fashion I have created a checklist and journal pages for 180 days, an entire school year! The pages will help with keeping you accountable to your self-care journey.

The chart is to record for what you do for selfcare. I have also included a journal for those who like to journal.

The idea behind the check list is simple each day you do some self-care for yourself shade or mark a square. The goal is you do something for 180 days, an entire school year and almost half of a year.

There are 4 charts with eighty boxes to equal 320 days of becoming a selfcare expert. Forty-five days short of a year.

There is also a journal section in the book, for those who like to journal on their journey of taking better care of themselves by participating in self-care every day. The journal section can be used as an independent journal to write what you did for selfcare, your thoughts, and feelings.

The journal and checklist are located at the end of the book. They can be removed from the book if you would like a separate journal.

About the Author

Renita Perry, native Missourian has been an Elementary Educator for over a score. She holds a Bachelor's and Master's Degree. She received recognition in Who's Who Among Teachers. She is part of the faculty at the National Baptist Congress of Christian Education. She is a member of Alpha Kappa Alpha Sorority Inc. When she's not writing, she's baking cookies, traveling to try new cuisine with her bestie, reading, shopping, walking, swimming, and spending time with family, friends. For self-care she walks to the corner and spends time on the patio enjoying the fresh air and her flower garden.

Visit her website at
Teachableresourcefullearners.com

Contact Information

I would love to know how you used the ideas on self-care in your own life and made them fit your needs.

Send pictures, videos, and/or emails to RenitaTRLConsults@gmail.com

Visit TeachableResourcefulLearners.com to learn more about our services and to schedule a training or inquire about speaking engagements on Self-Care.

To my encouragers, supporters, and purchasers I say thank you!

The School Year, 180 Days Accountability Pages

Checklists & Journal

My
Selfcare
Challenge
Charts

Check a box every day you
engage in self-care for yourself.

My Selfcare Challenge 1

1	2	3	4	5
6	7	8	9	10
11	12	13	14	15
16	17	18	19	20
21	22	23	24	25
26	27	28	29	30
31	32	33	34	35
36	37	38	39	40
41	42	43	44	45
46	47	48	49	50
51	52	53	54	55
56	57	58	59	60
61	62	63	64	65
66	67	68	69	70
71	72	73	74	75
76	77	78	79	80

My Selfcare Challenge 2

1	2	3	4	5
6	7	8	9	10
11	12	13	14	15
16	17	18	19	20
21	22	23	24	25
26	27	28	29	30
31	32	33	34	35
36	37	38	39	40
41	42	43	44	45
46	47	48	49	50
51	52	53	54	55
56	57	58	59	60
61	62	63	64	65
66	67	68	69	70
71	72	73	74	75
76	77	78	79	80

My Selfcare Challenge 3

1	2	3	4	5
6	7	8	9	10
11	12	13	14	15
16	17	18	19	20
21	22	23	24	25
26	27	28	29	30
31	32	33	34	35
36	37	38	39	40
41	42	43	44	45
46	47	48	49	50
51	52	53	54	55
56	57	58	59	60
61	62	63	64	65
66	67	68	69	70
71	72	73	74	75
76	77	78	79	80

My Selfcare Challenge 4

1	2	3	4	5
6	7	8	9	10
11	12	13	14	15
16	17	18	19	20
21	22	23	24	25
26	27	28	29	30
31	32	33	34	35
36	37	38	39	40
41	42	43	44	45
46	47	48	49	50
51	52	53	54	55
56	57	58	59	60
61	62	63	64	65
66	67	68	69	70
71	72	73	74	75
76	77	78	79	80

How to use the Journal

A self-care journal is a journal that you use to write about your emotions, feelings, thoughts and reflections in a healthy way that will make yourself feel better.

Journal about 10-15 minutes for 3-5 days a week. Use journal prompts to help you get started or just reflect on your self-care.

Suggested Prompts for Journaling
What does a perfect self-care day look like?
How can you celebrate you today?
What went well for me today?
What can I do to make tomorrow better?
How do I recharge?
What makes me feel calm?
Today I am grateful for?
Today for self-care I did.
Today I feel?

Benefits of Journaling
Clarifies thoughts and feelings
Reduces stress, anxiety, and trauma
Increases emotional intelligence
Clears feelings of confusion or misdirection
Boosts motivation and self confidence
Provides support for depression
Improves sleep, memory, and mood

_____'s

180 Days
Self-Care
Challenge
Journal

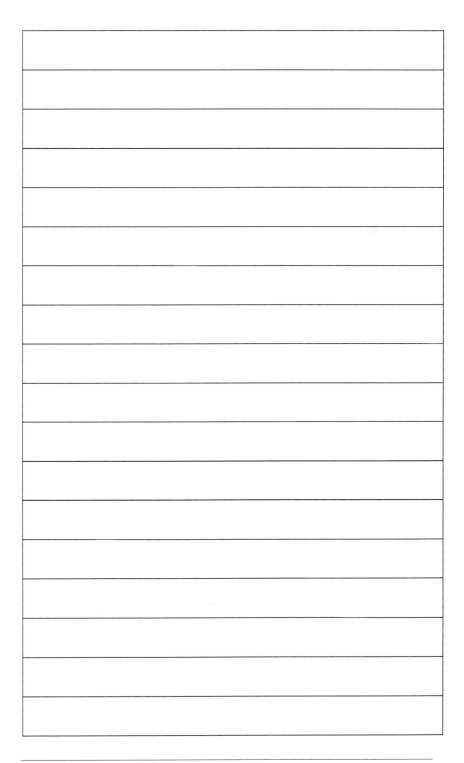

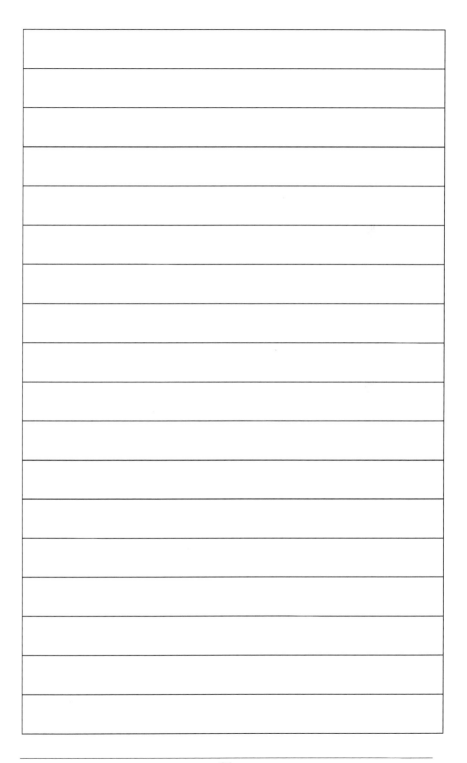

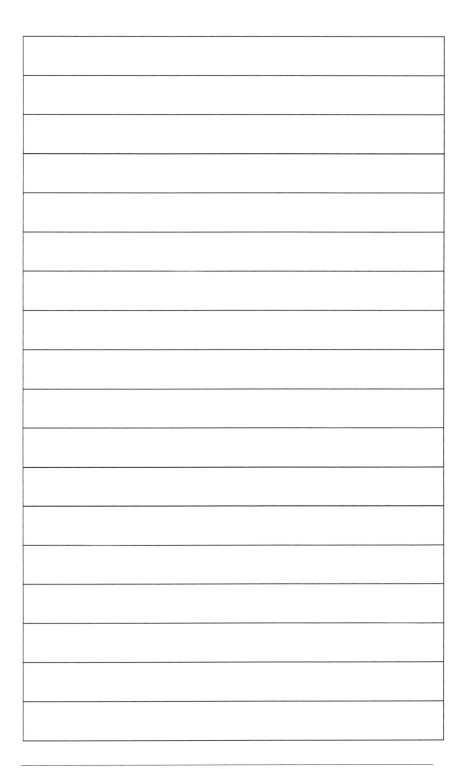